Other Books By The Author

Winner for Best Inspirational in Pacific Book Award 2020

RICHARD BYRD

JUST A THOUGHT

Volume IV

Just A Thought
Volume IV

Copyright © 2022 by Richard Byrd.

Paperback ISBN: 978-1-63812-440-5
Ebook ISBN: 978-1-63812-441-2

All rights reserved. No part in this book may be produced and transmitted in any form or by any means, electronic, or mechanical, including photocopying, recording, or by any information storage and retrieval system, without permission in writing from the copyright owner.

The views expressed in this work are solely those of the author and do not necessarily reflect the views of the publisher hereby disclaims any responsibility for them.

Published by Pen Culture Solutions 09/14/2022

Pen Culture Solutions
1-888-727-7204 (USA)
1-800-950-458 (Australia)
support@penculturesolutions.com

Just a thought IV

Some of the best relationships consist of just lovers and friends... just a thought

You cannot receive
your best answers
from yourself ...
Just a thought

*Do you have the
nerve to be more
than you think
that you can be ...
Just a thought*

Always hold back your anger because it is better to put out a little fire than to allow the whole forest to burn ... Just a thought

Do not boast about what you will do tomorrow because nobody knows what tomorrow will bring forth ... Just a thought

Never allow fear
to hijack you from
seeking out your
next new endeavor...
Just a thought

*The mind knows
what the heart
should remember
... Just a thought*

*Every day may not
be a good day but it's
a good day to wake
up amongst the living
... Just a thought*

Always remember that if pretty was a picture, then you would be the whole roll of film ... Just a thought

Keep in mind that the person that you are taking for granted, somewhere someone else is praying to have ... Just a thought

*The past isn't ours
to change but today
is ours to create ...
Just a thought*

Doors automatically opens when GOD gives you favor ... Just a thought

Even broken halos
can be repaired ...
Just a thought

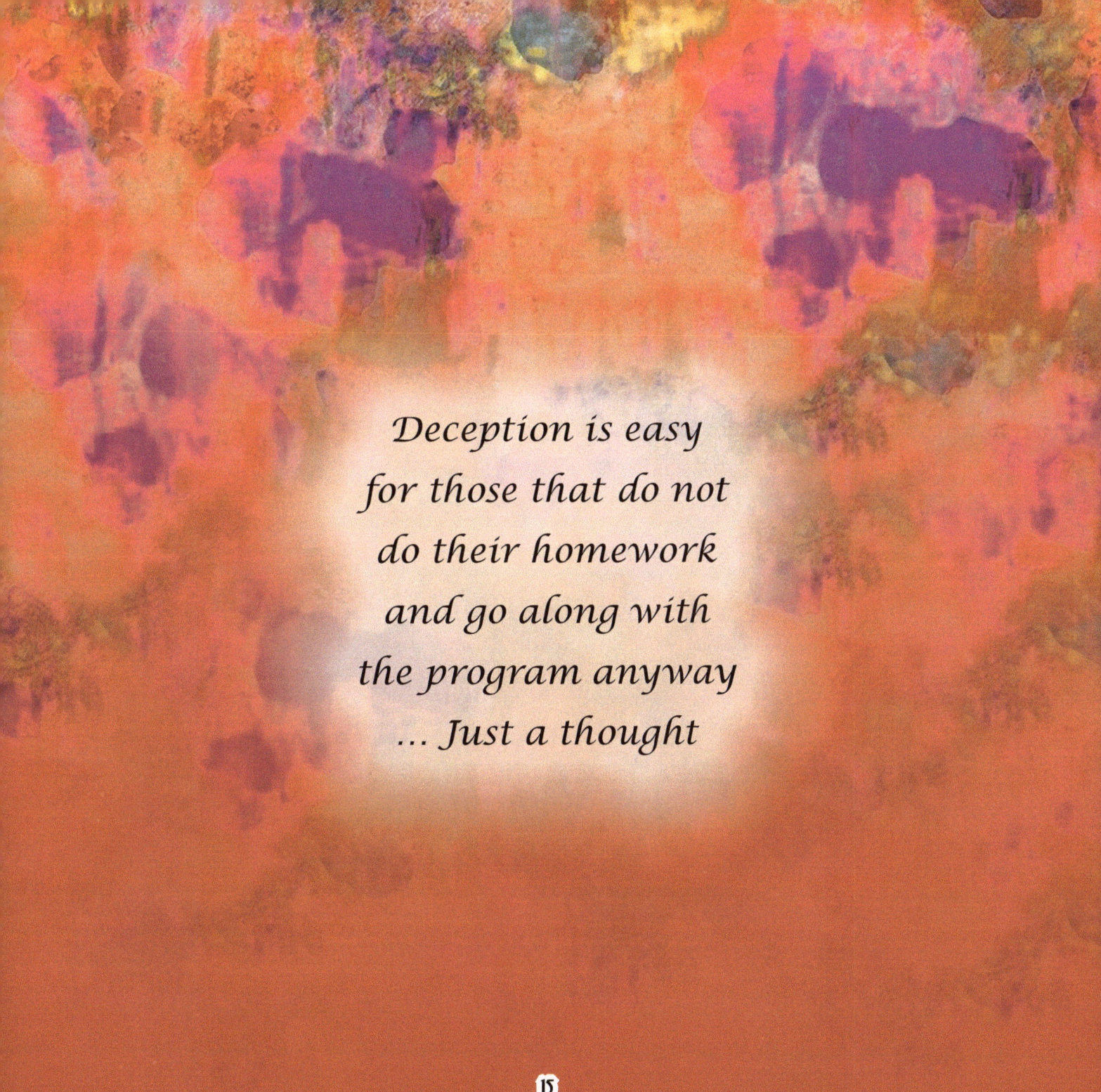

*Deception is easy
for those that do not
do their homework
and go along with
the program anyway
... Just a thought*

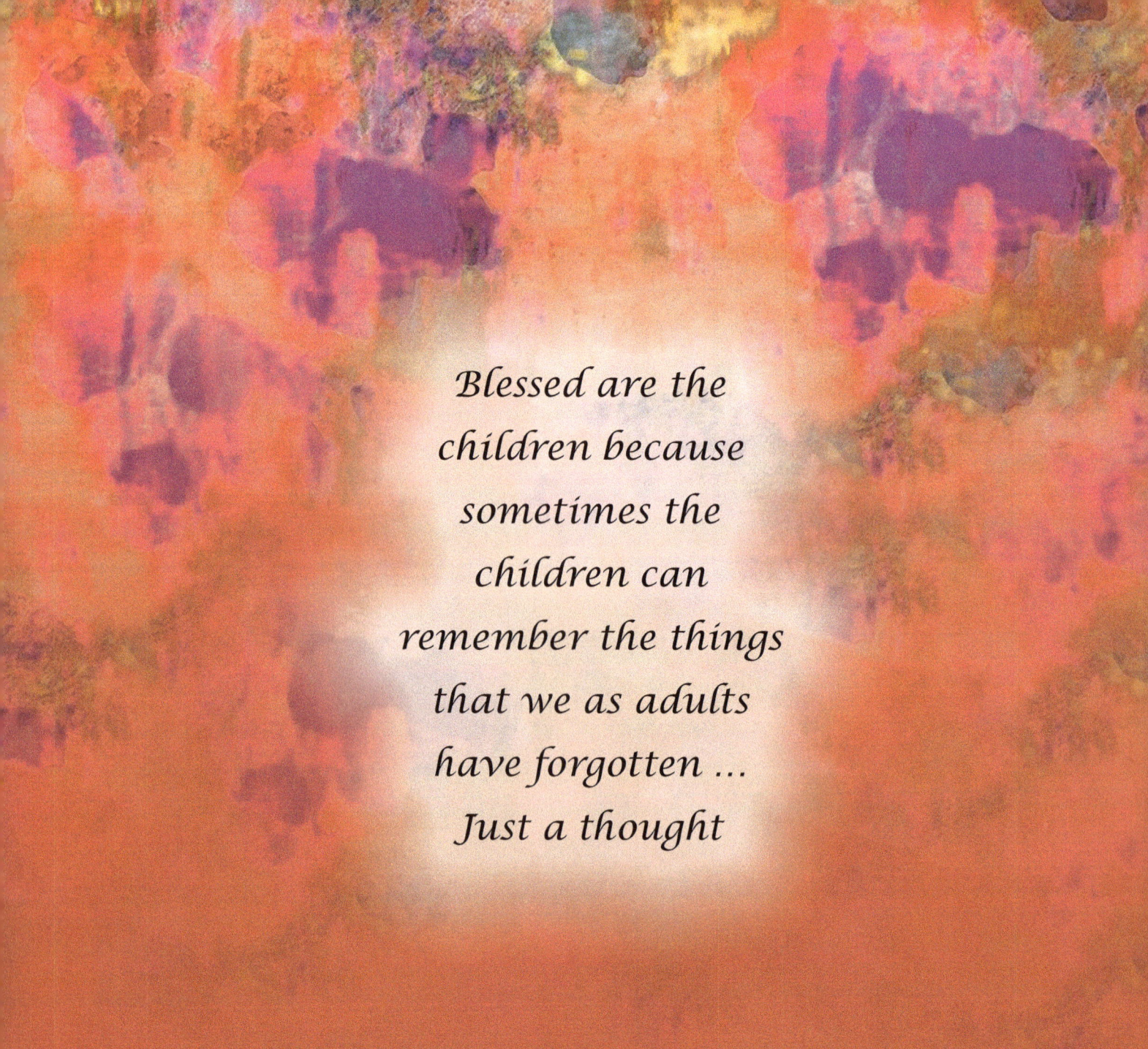

Blessed are the children because sometimes the children can remember the things that we as adults have forgotten ... Just a thought

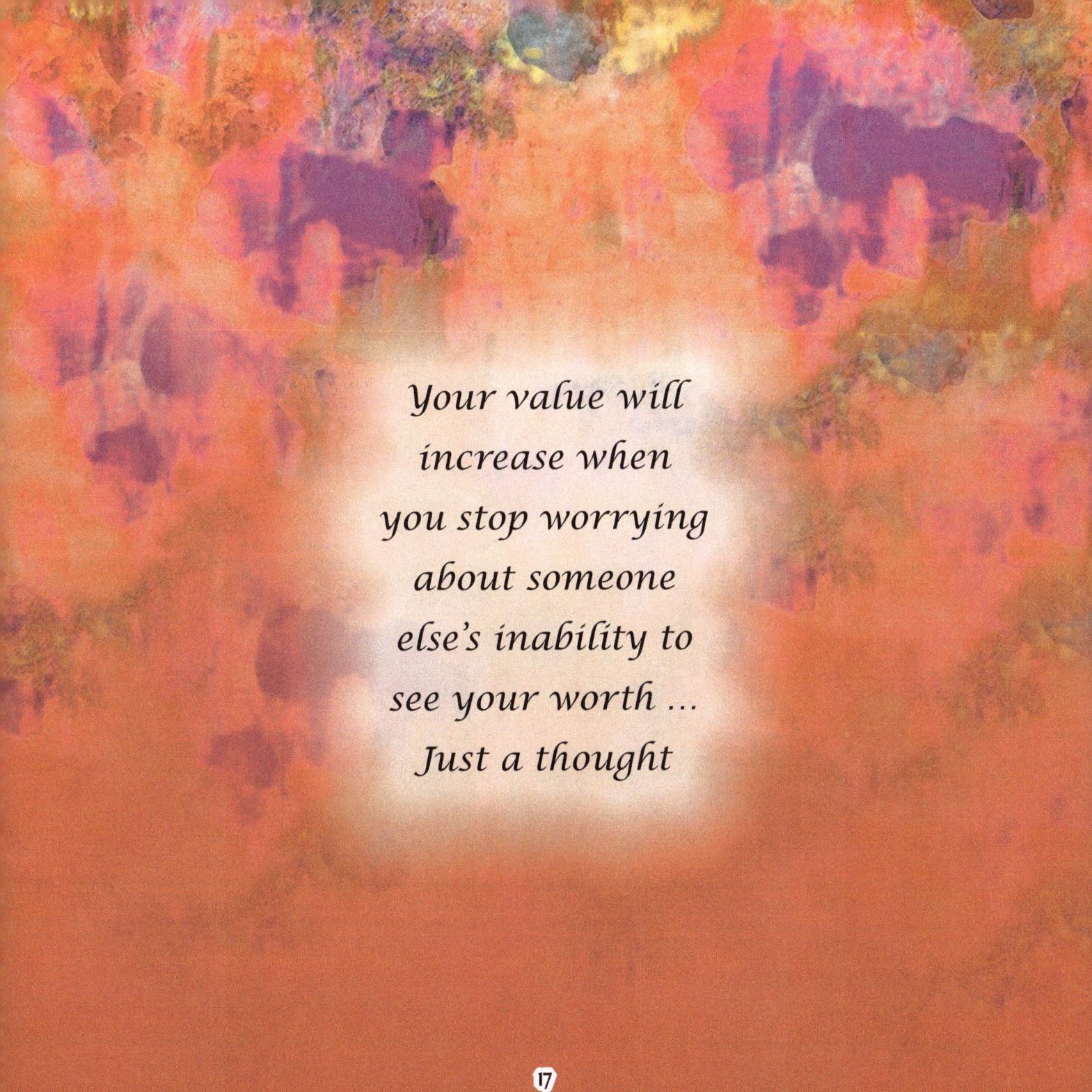

Your value will
increase when
you stop worrying
about someone
else's inability to
see your worth ...
Just a thought

Stay prepare for the unknown ... Just a thought

You may see the same stars in the sky but the roads below your feet have changed... Just a thought

Action will always speak louder than any words can say ... Just a thought

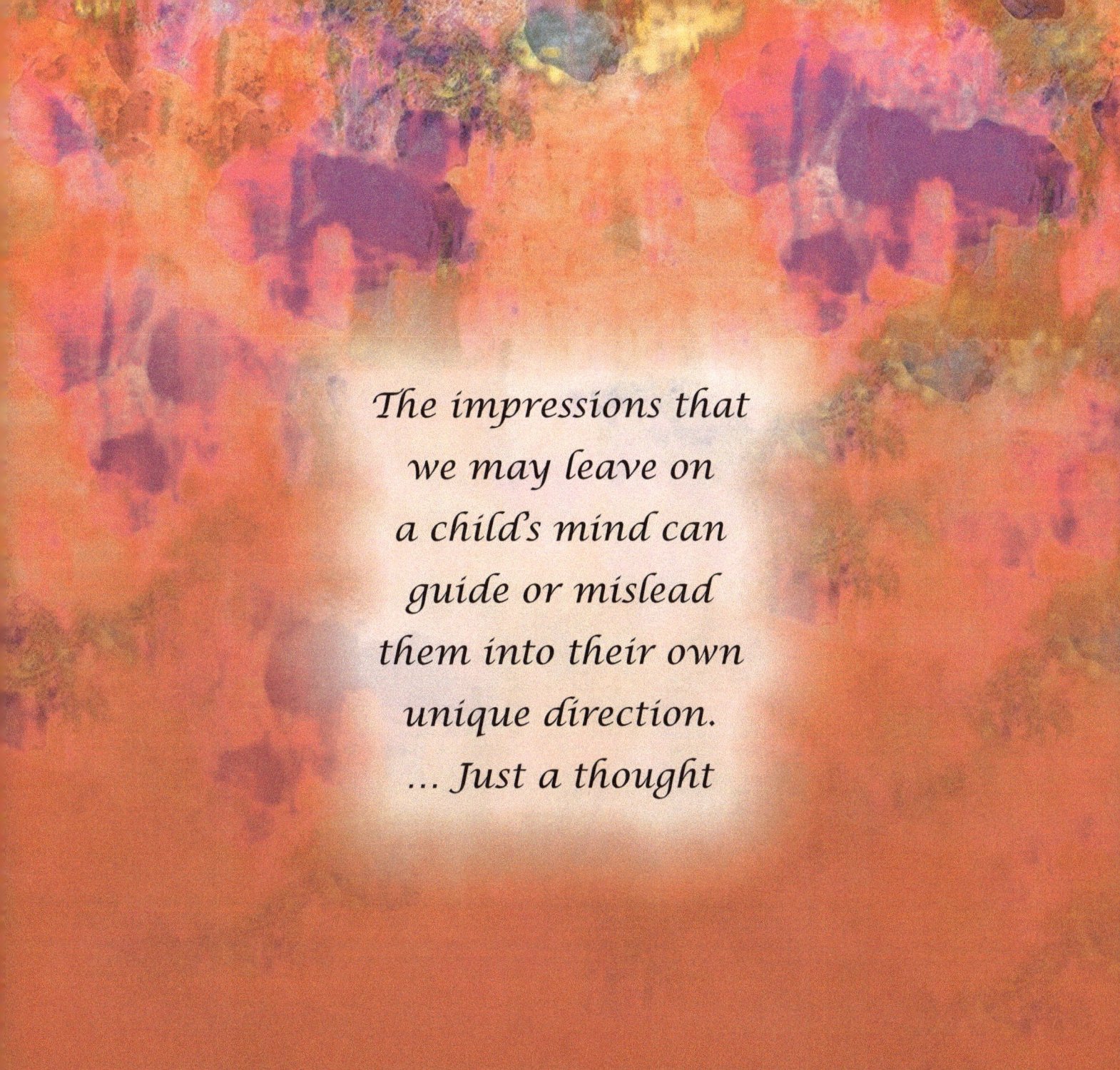

The impressions that we may leave on a child's mind can guide or mislead them into their own unique direction.
... Just a thought

In this physical realm we must remember that the material things of this world will always be temporary ... Just a thought

*Without a command,
concern or argument
is giving a suggestion
… Just a thought*

Limitations are only here so that we can move beyond them ... Just a thought

*Right or wrong begins
with your perception
on the matter...
Just a thought*

Chaos and destruction are very noisy, but forgiveness and peace are silent, people don't always need to hear what's on your mind ... Just a thought

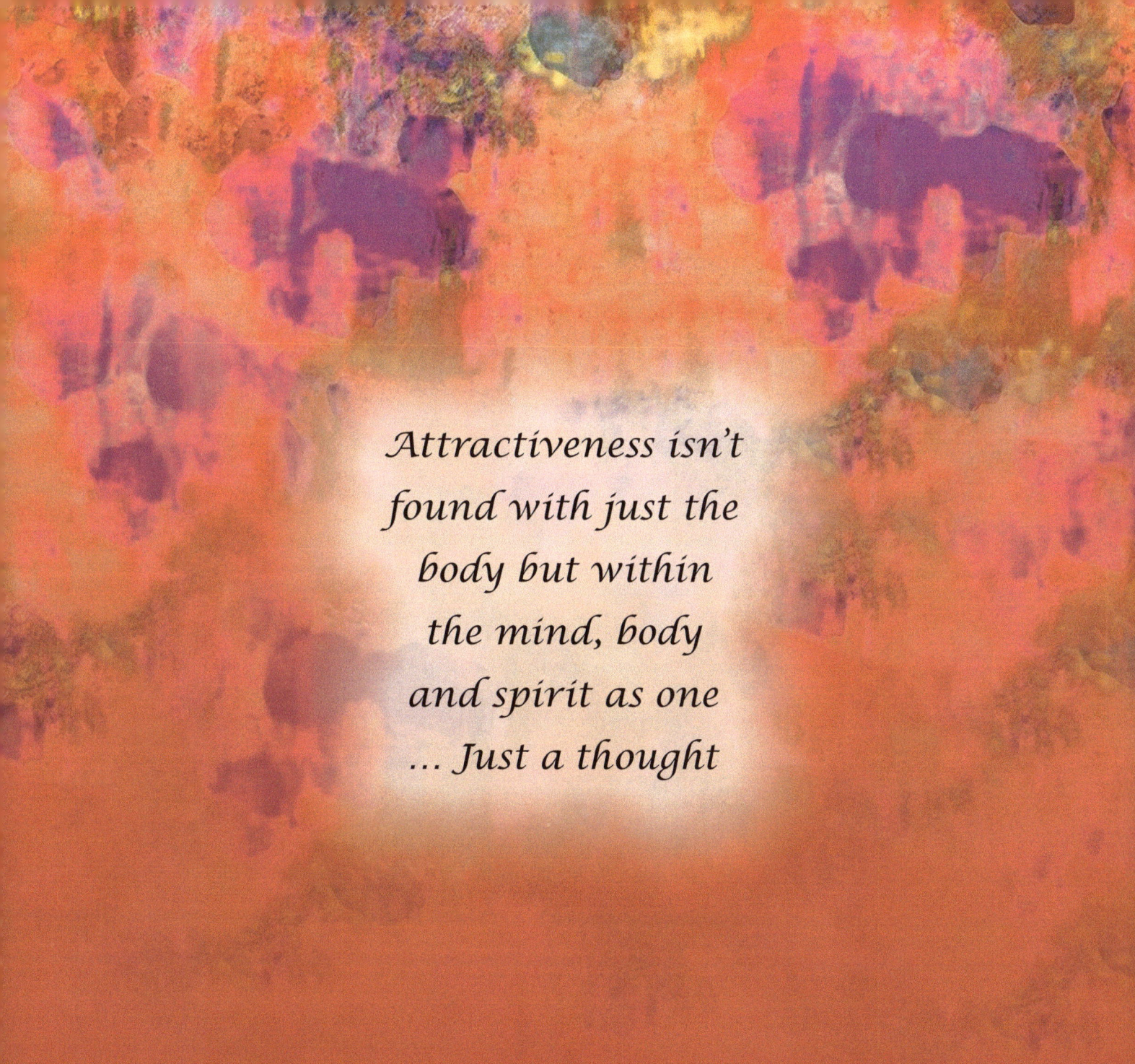

Attractiveness isn't found with just the body but within the mind, body and spirit as one ... Just a thought

If ignorance equaled awareness, then we all would be lost ... Just a thought

*Don't allow anyone
the option to put
you down, your
value is greater
than you may think
… Just a thought*

She doesn't have to have the whole world she just needs to know that she's the most important person in yours ...
Just a thought

Many are blinded by
lust which only sees
itself as fresh love
... Just a thought

*You don't stop living
when you get old,
you get old when
you stop living …
Just a thought*

Your struggles may
be like a brick wall
until you, decide
to get over them.
... just a thought

Take action over the words or just put the words into action ... Just a thought

Don't be to ambitious and always keep your priorities in mind ... Just a thought

Some people do to much even though its still not enough ... Just a thought

*Just because it may
be difficult to achieve
it, this does not mean
that it cannot be done
… Just a thought*

We all have problems
that we must deal
with but where
there's a problem
there's a solution
... Just a thought

*Divine peace is
a reality that
most people will
never know ...
Just a thought*

What's between
the world and you
besides you are
finding yourself in
it ... Just a thought

Life is like going to school sometimes we don't understand the lesson until we have failed the examination ... Just a thought

Your burdens are greatly increased when you invite them in ... Just a thought

Never try to change anyone, just reevaluate your own position ... Just a thought

You have not because
you asked not, and
money cannot buy
you a miracle ...
Just a thought

Subscribe to the rest of your life ... Just a thought

Remember to always
do your best even
if nobody gives you
any credit for it ...
Just a thought

It's possible for us to go from strangers to friends when we are willing to interact ... Just a thought

We all have a beginning and an end, what we do in-between is a choice ... Just a thought

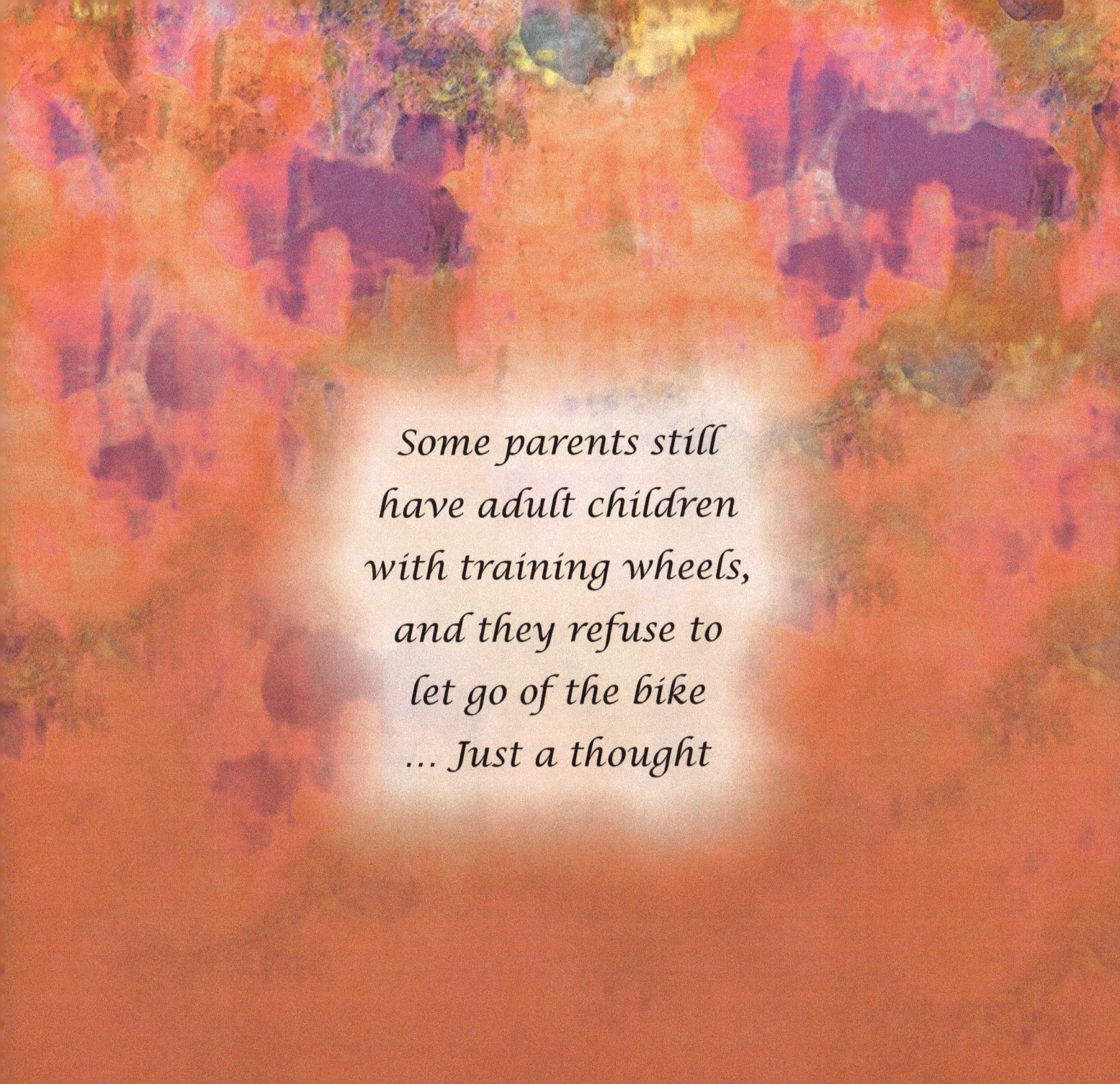

Some parents still have adult children with training wheels, and they refuse to let go of the bike ... Just a thought

It doesn't hurt to laugh at your mistakes especially when the relationship is over ... Just a thought

Sometimes life will remove people that you never thought of losing just to replace them with someone that you always dreamed of having ... Just a thought

Nice words are not always true and true words are not always nice ... Just a thought

Only with those good
old friends, the ones
that's still around can
you find a lifetime
of forgotten words
... Just a thought

You can make
imperfection look
good, strong look
powerful and
the weight of
the world feel as
light as a feather
when you have a
positive attitude
... Just a thought

Secret admirers
come in many forms,
but the best forms
are still a secret ...
Just a thought

Desire will sneak up on you and it doesn't wait for the right time ... Just a thought

Love may arrive amongst dependency and lust, but it doesn't have to remain that way ... Just a thought

A great speaker can move many, but a great writer will hold their attention … Just a thought

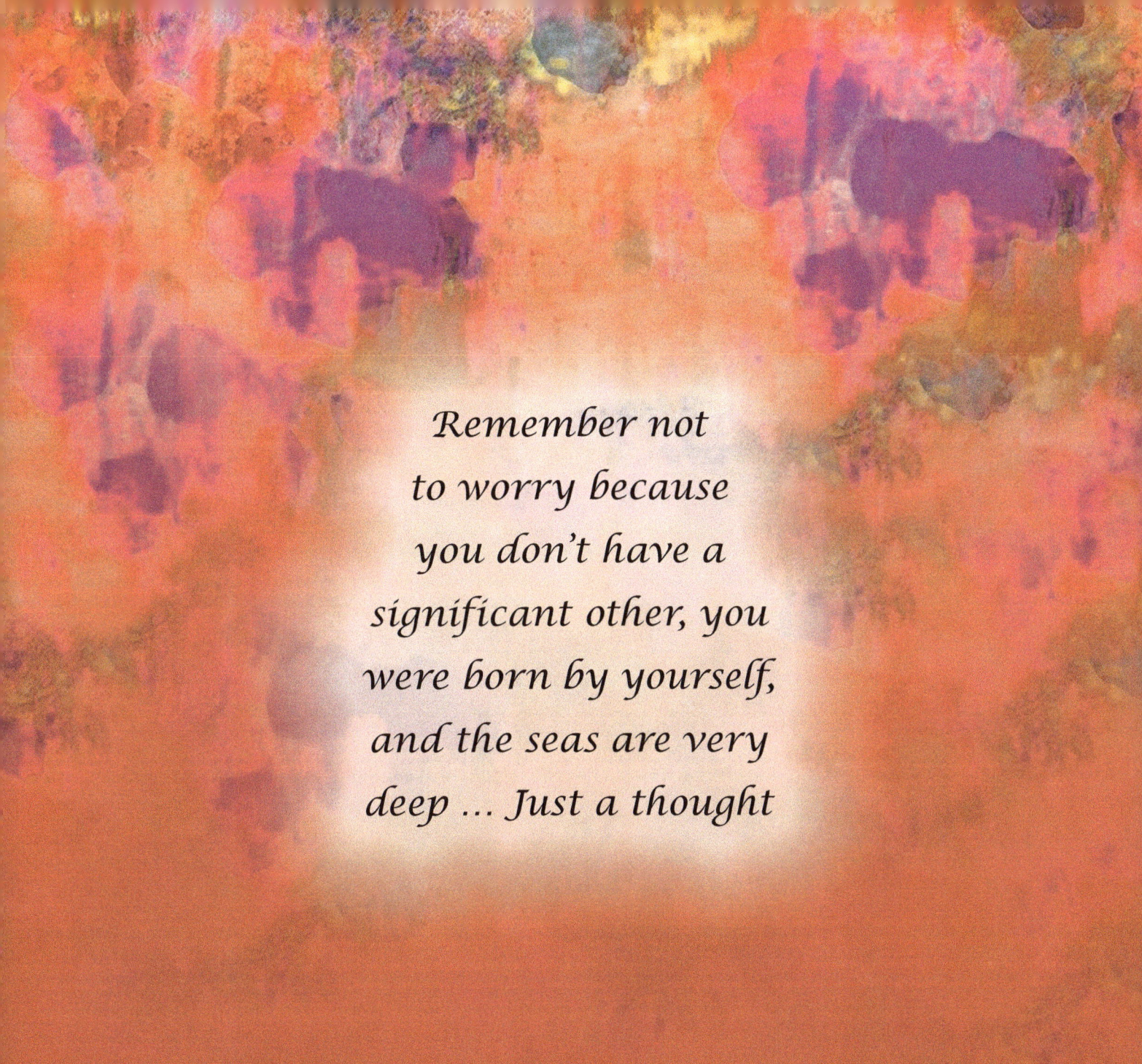

Remember not
to worry because
you don't have a
significant other, you
were born by yourself,
and the seas are very
deep ... Just a thought

*It takes more
strength to hold on
to something than it
does to just let it go
… Just a thought*

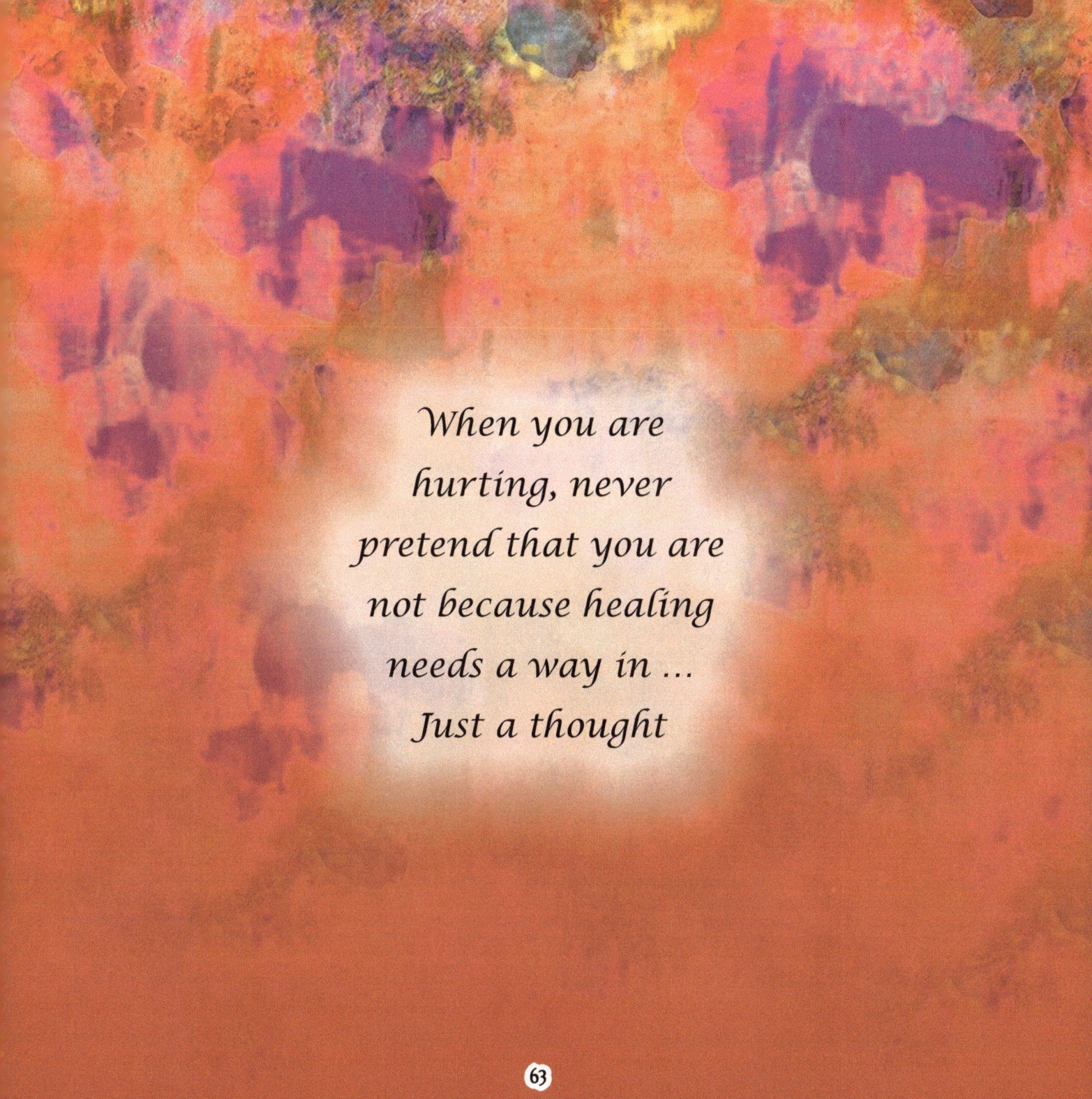

When you are hurting, never pretend that you are not because healing needs a way in ... Just a thought

Revenge and justice will sometimes straddle the same fence ... Just a thought

*Did you think
it or did you do
the research ...
Just a thought*

Never confuse what you can do and what you won't do ... Just a thought

Curiosity may have killed the cat, but it didn't stop the mouse from sneaking around ... Just a thought

*Even when they
don't tell you what's
on their mind,
listen anyway …
Just a thought*

Your enabler isn't helping ... Just a thought

We may all be able
to stand on our own
2 feet, but we must
interact with someone
to reach our goals
... Just a thought

You can care and love someone with every part of your being and still be glad that he or she are no longer a part of your life ... Just a thought

*Inner peace comes
when you are happy
with yourself...
Just a thought*

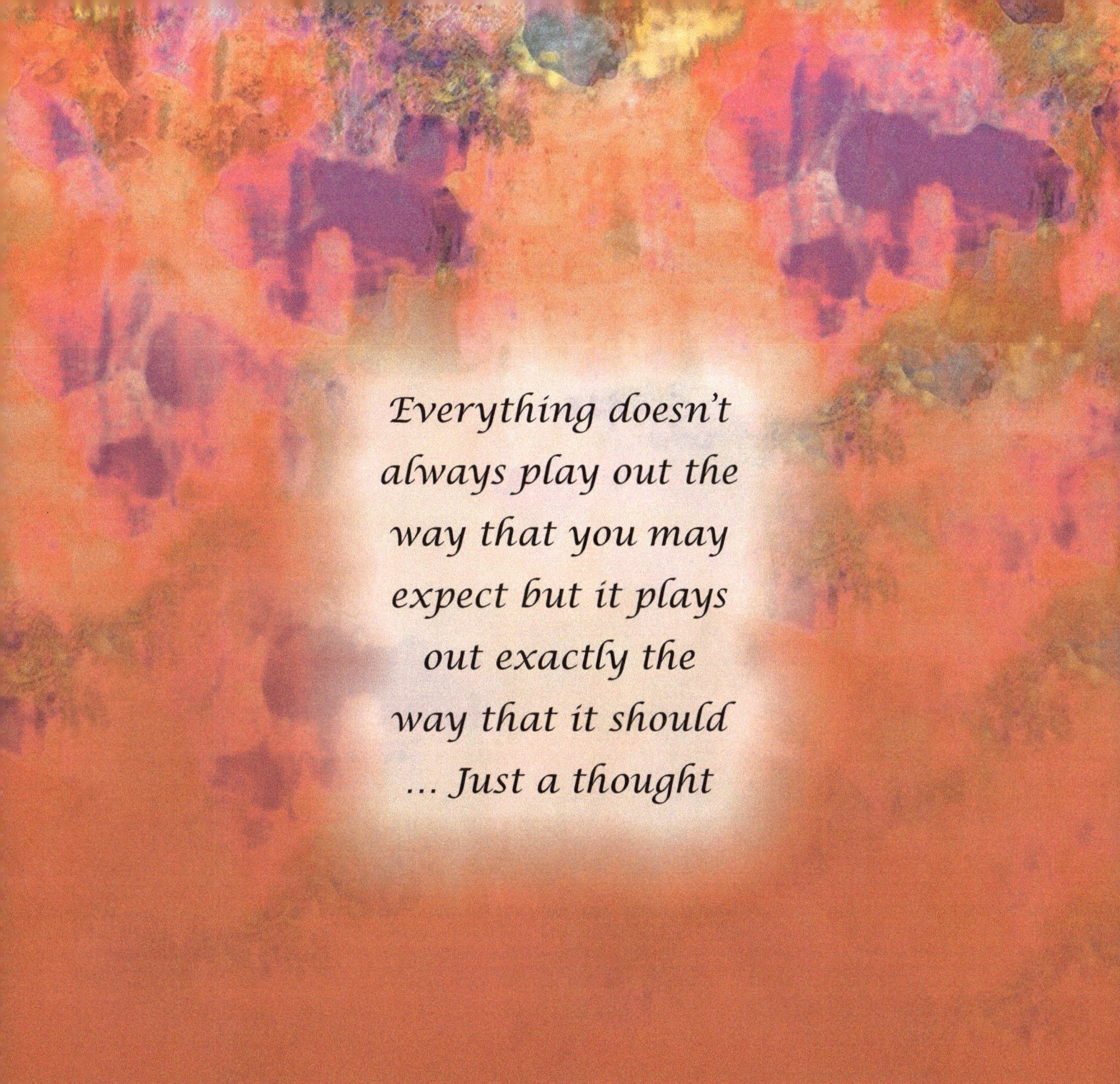

Everything doesn't always play out the way that you may expect but it plays out exactly the way that it should ... Just a thought

*Some people think
that they are
starting from scratch
without realizing
that they can never
scratch away their
own experiences
... Just a thought*

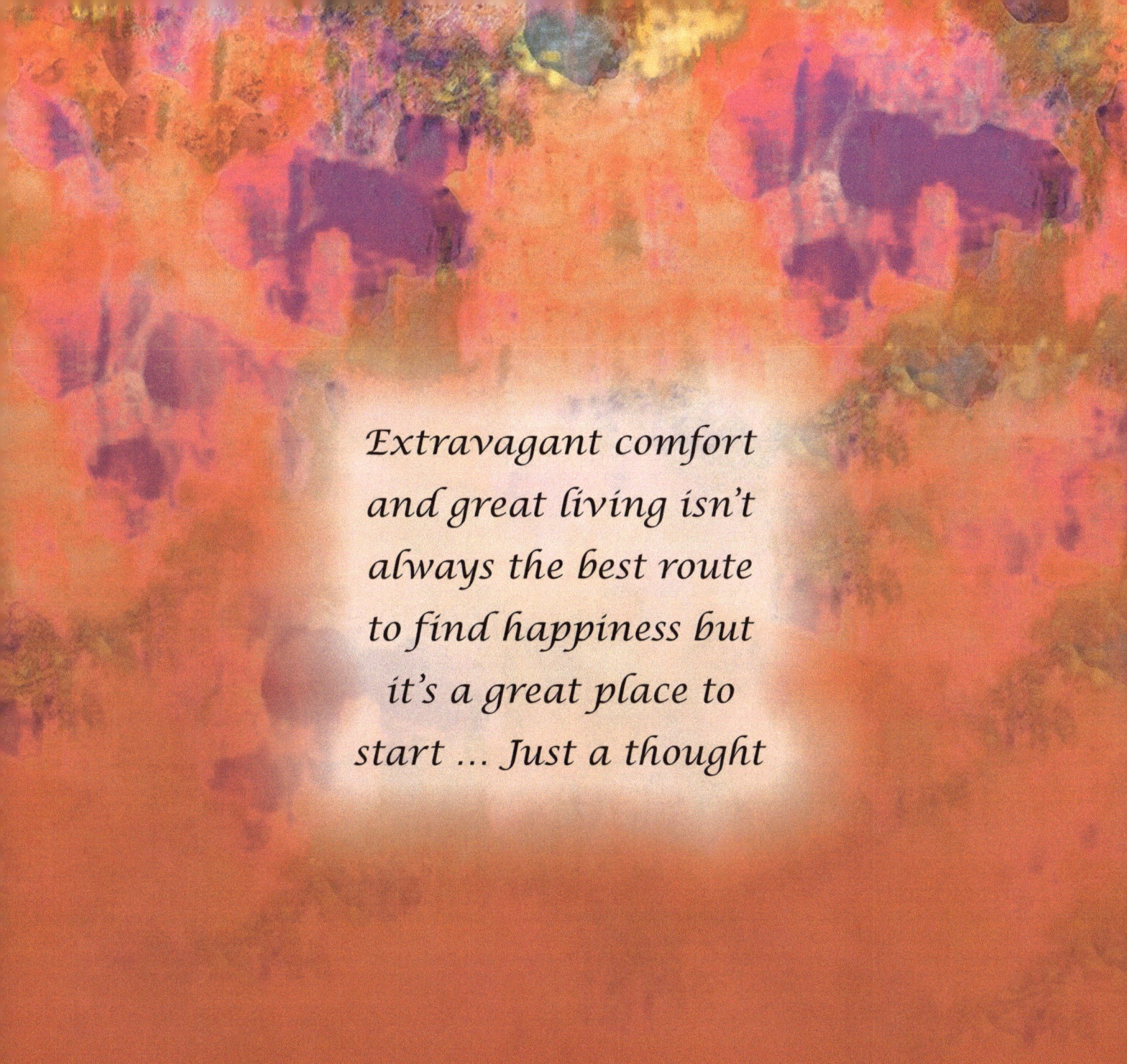

Extravagant comfort and great living isn't always the best route to find happiness but it's a great place to start ... Just a thought

If he or she sleeps on your couch with no job, eats your food and pays no rent then you just may have welcomed in a squatter ... Just a thought

Sometimes it only
takes one person
to smile to make
another person's day
... Just a thought

A long awaited achievement along with compliments and cheers walks on the same road towards congratulations ...
Just a thought

Everyone loves a rose
only after the thorns
has been removed
… Just a thought

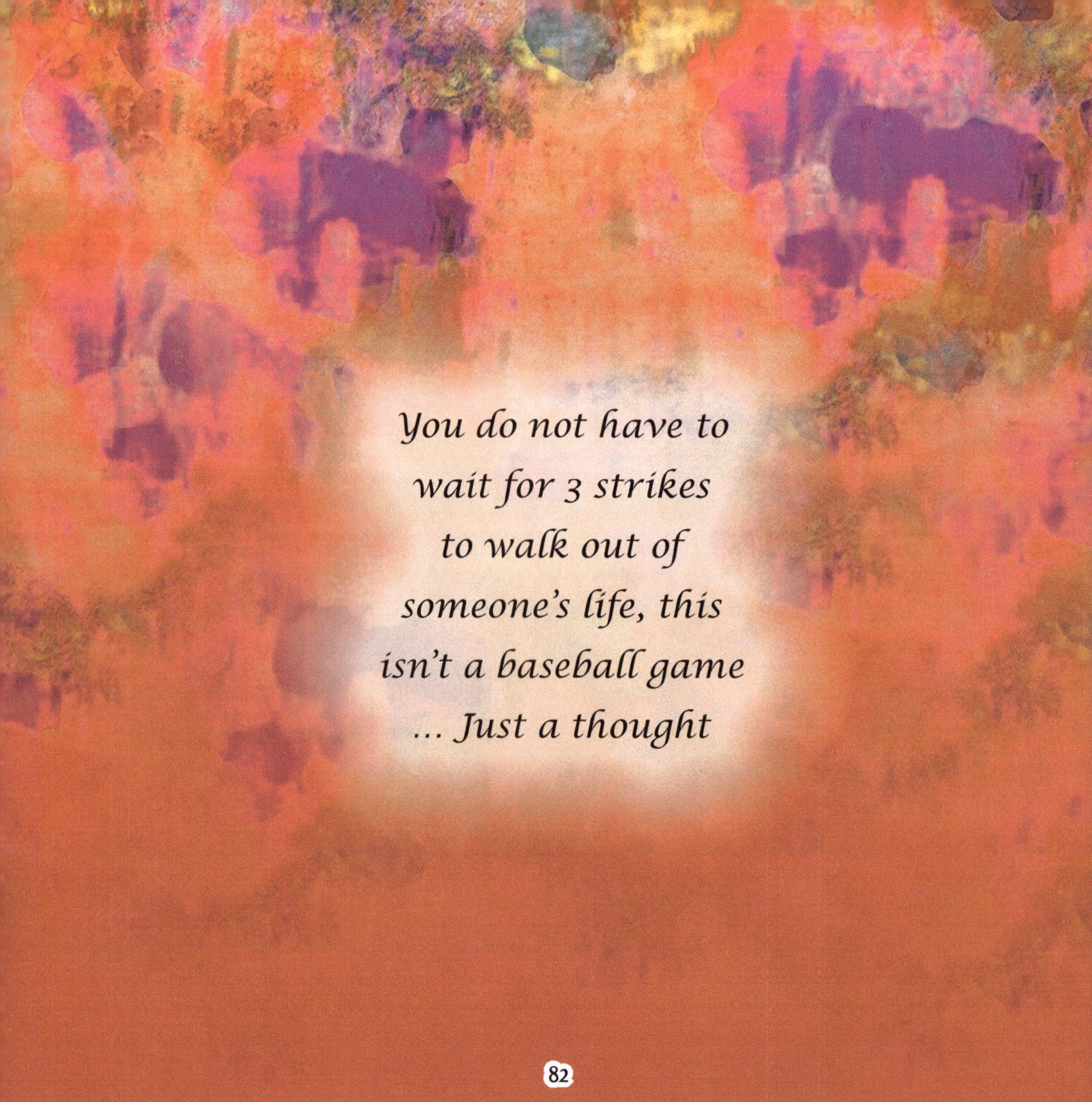

You do not have to wait for 3 strikes to walk out of someone's life, this isn't a baseball game ... Just a thought

Society may be an ugly mess, but you do not have to join the team ... Just a thought

They may be attractive, alluring or enticing but temptation has many faces ... Just a thought

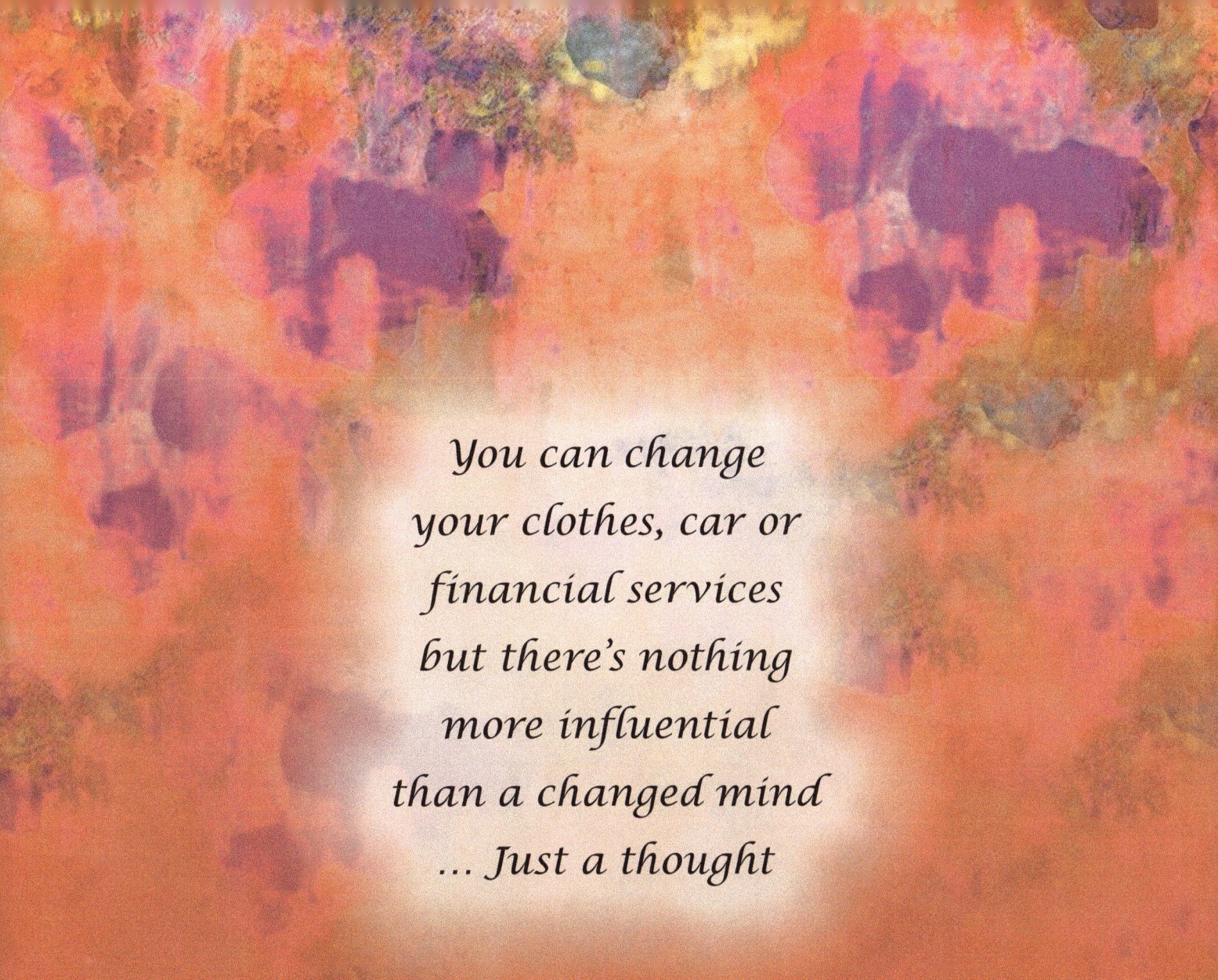

You can change your clothes, car or financial services but there's nothing more influential than a changed mind ... Just a thought

A miracle requires
no prescription ...
Just a thought

Every life has a beginning, a middle and an end so be kind to one another in the middle ... Just a thought

At the end of the day,
the most important
thing to know is that
you've done your best
… Just a thought

When we think of
visions that we may
not see, we think
of the children and
all the possibilities
... Just a thought

If you were not invited or considered then don't be bothered, your steps may be redirected for a greater purpose ... Just a thought

Regardless of how often you may clean up a trash can, it's still a trash can ... Just a thought

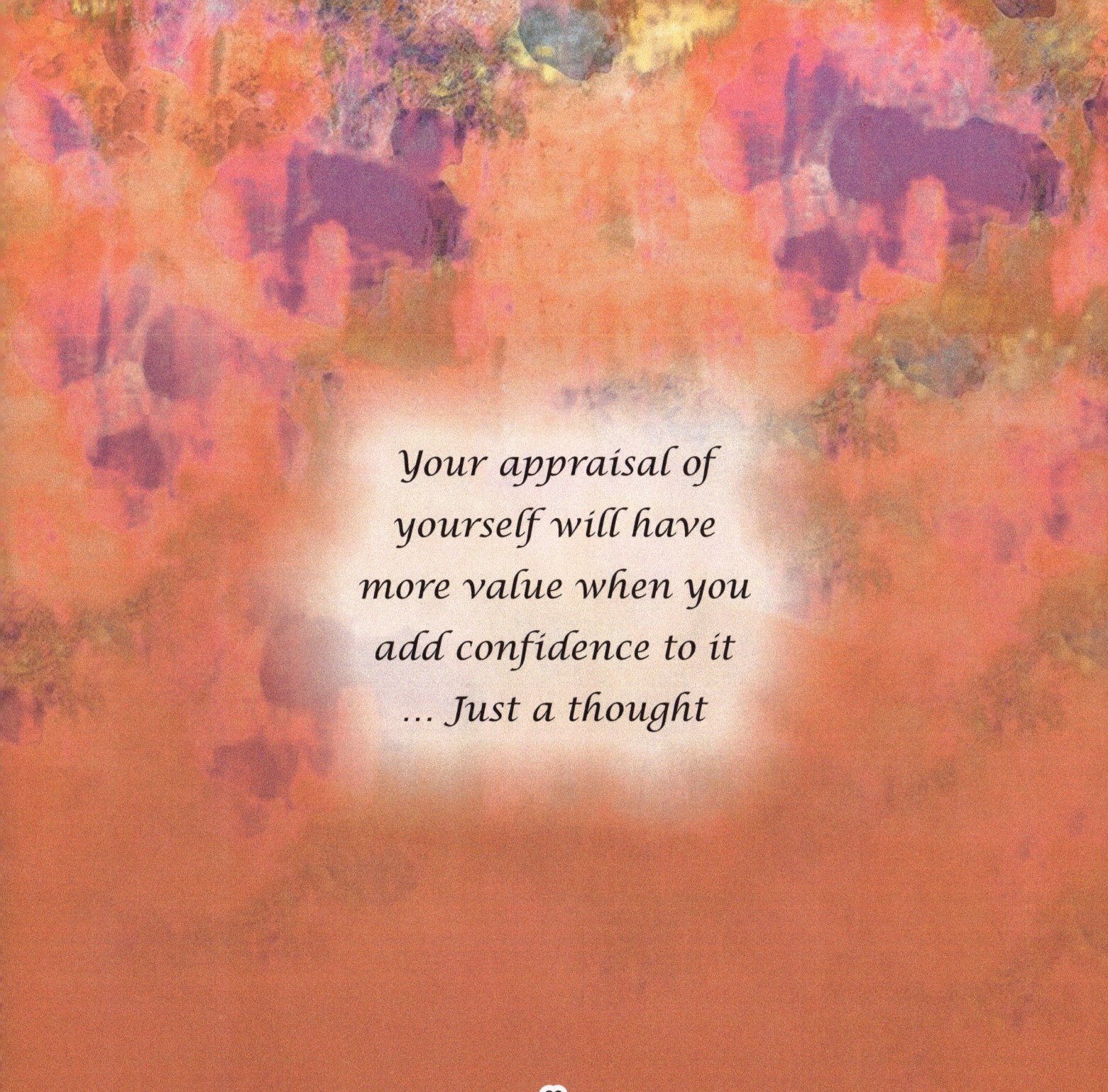

Your appraisal of yourself will have more value when you add confidence to it … Just a thought

You are moving in
the right direction
if someone see's
your signature as
an autograph ...
Just a thought

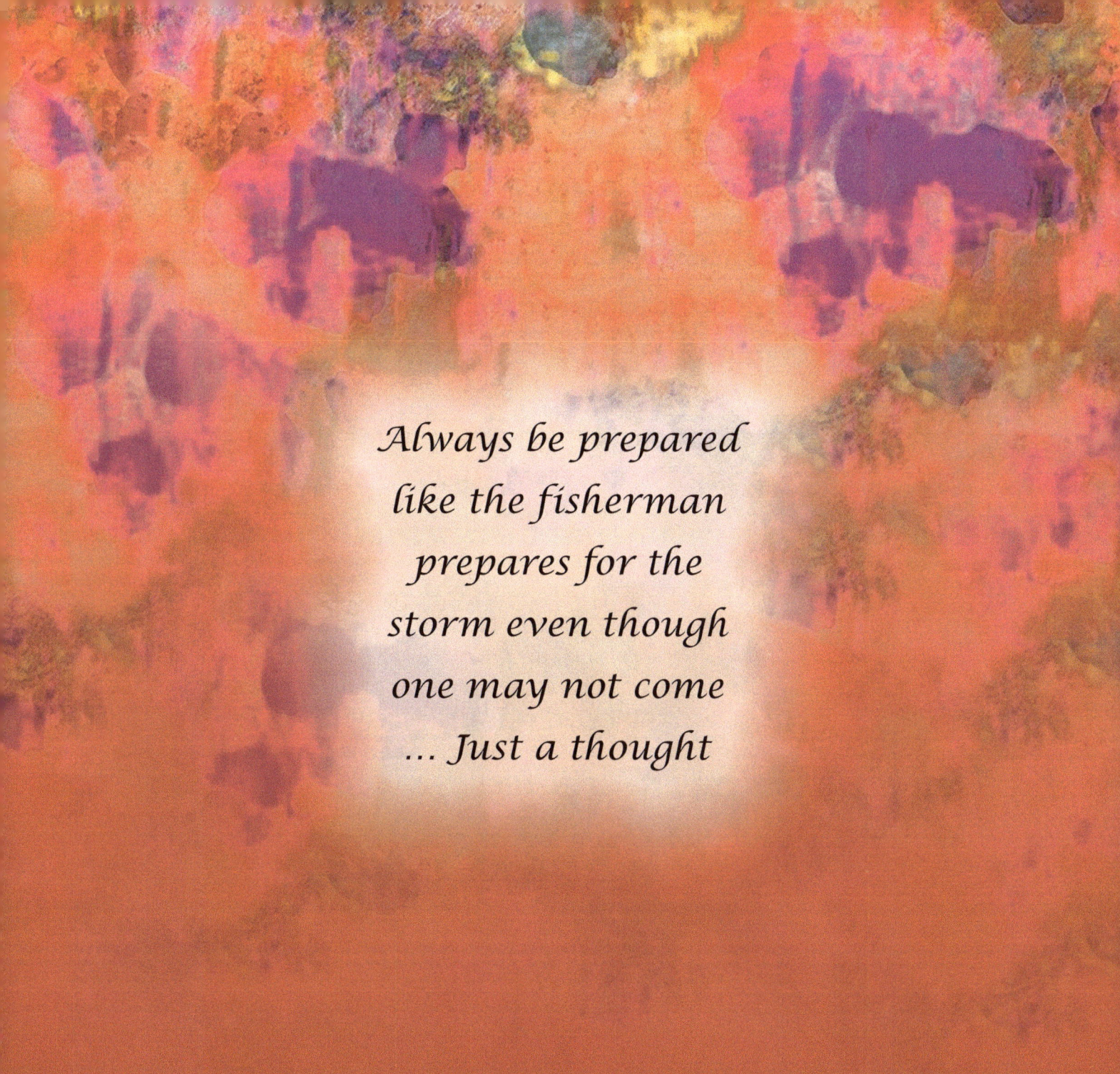

Always be prepared like the fisherman prepares for the storm even though one may not come ... Just a thought

While you are in
a relationship,
situations will tell
you if you have
a companion or
just company ...
Just a thought

Even if you are cracked in a 1000 places, you must know that you are not broken beyond repair ... Just a thought

Sometimes people like to think that they are more important than the next person, but which spoke is more important on the wheel ... Just a thought

*Pause for a moment, your
moved swings are only
temporary
indecisions of thought...
just a thought*

ABOUT THE AUTHOR

Richard Byrd debuts in the literary limelight with the release of "Just A Thought" (published by AuthorHouse in July 2018). Inspired from his personal experiences, the self-help book that is set for a new marketing push, aims to motivate others and elevate them into their own unique direction.

In "Just A Thought," Byrd offers readers quotes and thoughts that would inspire them, ease their stress and motivate them to a positive direction. Moreover, he emphasizes how the book can help anyone to translate knowledge into reasonable and good decisions.